D1714479

100 Dates with Jesus

ONE HUNDRED UNCONVENTIONAL WAYS TO STRENGTHEN
YOUR RELATIONSHIP WITH JESUS!

STEPHANIE ALEXIS BURREL

Copyright © 2022 by Stephanie Alexis Burrel

All rights reserved. No part of this publication may be reproduced, distributed, or transmitted in any form or by any means, including photocopying, recording, or other electronic or mechanical methods, without the prior written permission of the publisher, except in the case of brief quotations embodied in critical reviews and certain other noncommercial uses permitted by copyright law. For permission requests, write to the author via the website, or email stephaniealexisauthor@gmail.com.

Editing and typesetting: Sally Hanan at Inksnatcher.com
Cover Design: Nirosha at Printok

All Scripture quotations are taken from The Holy Bible, New International Version®, ®. Copyright ©1973, 1978, 1984, 2011 by Biblica, Inc.™ Used by permission of Zondervan. All rights reserved worldwide. www.zondervan.com

Scripture quotations marked (NKJV) are taken from the New King James Version®. Copyright © 1982 by Thomas Nelson. Used by permission. All rights reserved.

Scripture quotations marked (NASB) are taken from the New American Standard Bible ®, Copyright © 1960, 1962, 1963, 1968, 1971, 1972, 1973, 1975, 1977, 1995 by The Lockman Foundation. Used by permission.

Scripture quotations marked (ESV) are from The Holy Bible, English Standard Version ® (ESV ®), copyright © 2001 by Crossway, a publishing ministry of Good News Publishers. Used by permission. All rights reserved.

Scripture quotations marked (NLT) are taken from the *Holy Bible, New Living Translation,* copyright © 1996, 2004, 2007, 2013 by Tyndale House Foundation. Used by permission of Tyndale House Publishers, Inc., Carol Stream, Illinois 60188. All rights reserved.

Scripture quotations marked TPT are from The Passion Translation®. Copyright © 2017, 2018 by Passion & Fire Ministries, Inc. Used by permission. All rights reserved. ThePassionTranslation.com.

Ordering Information: Quantity sales. Special discounts are available on quantity purchases by corporations, associations, and others. For details, contact the author at the email address above.

100 Dates with Jesus/Stephanie Burrel

ISBN

Hardback 9798422532957

Paperback 9798429090412

To the beloved, chosen before the foundation of the universe was laid, woven together in love by love, Himself. May you continue to fall deeper in love with Jesus, the Anointed One.

Contents

Intro

In this book you will discover one hundred fun, new ways to fellowship with Jesus. You will come to understand what it truly means to be His precious bride, the beloved. Through a variety of spontaneous, heartwarming dates, you will unlock a level of intimacy with Him that is sure to transform your life.

Jesus doesn't want to be a distant friend you spend time with a few times per week. Instead, He wants to be a trustworthy confidant you learn to abide in and depend on.

Through every date, you'll come to understand Him deeper and really see why He chose to give up His life for you. You'll come to know Him as a brother, Father, companion, helper, and friend.

Your series of adventures start now!

Buckle up and enjoy the ride.

Please feel free to hashtag #100dateswithJesus in any photos or videos that you post on social media from your dates! Or send us your videos and photos via email to stephaniealexisauthor@gmail.com. We would love to see all of the exciting things you and Jesus are doing!

Hearing from Jesus

You were designed to hear from Jesus. As His sheep, you hear His voice (John 10:27). One of the things I love about Jesus is that He speaks to us in many different ways.

- ✓ Some people are hearers. Hearers might be on their morning walk or at the grocery store and hear Jesus speak a word to their heart.

- ✓ Others hear from Jesus through feeling. Feelers can sense Jesus's emotions of pleasure or sadness.

- ✓ Others hear from Jesus by knowing. These individuals have an internal sense of knowing when Jesus is near, and of what He wants to communicate to them.

- ✓ Then there are seers. Seers hear Jesus through dreams and visions. A seer might get a picture in their mind of something symbolic that Jesus wants to convey to them or through them.

Whether you are a hearer, feeler, knower, or seer, the more you practice hearing from Jesus, the more you'll find that distinguishing His voice from the voices around you will become much easier.

Date 1

Coffee with the King

Look! I stand at the door and knock. If you hear
my voice and open the door, I will come in, and
we will share a meal together as friends.
—Revelation 3:20 NLT

Today you'll be having coffee with Jesus! He's had this on the books in heaven for a while now. Grab your trusty journal and a great ink pen and head over to your favorite local coffee shop. Order your drink and find a nice comfy, cozy spot to hang out with Him. As you sit together enjoying one another's company,

— Ask Him —

- How do you see me?
- What are you wanting to teach me today?
- How can I love you better?

Date 2

Carpool Karaoke

I am faithful to you, and you can trust me. I will sing and play music for you, my God.
—Psalm 57:7 CEV

Do you ever find yourself in the car singing at the top of your lungs, blasting your favorite tunes, imagining you're one of the finalists on *American Idol?* We've all got that special playlist or song that brings back happy memories from our past. Today's date, carpool karaoke, will be an exciting date that steers you in the right direction. (Get it, steer? LOL)

Before you head out and jump in the car, I want you to create a playlist composed of six songs. Ask Him to pick His three favorites, and you do the same. Then get in your car and go for a thirty-minute ride together.

— Ask Him —

- What did you enjoy most about our date today?

Date 3

Evening Walk

Your ears shall hear a word behind you, saying,
'This is the way, walk in it,' when you turn to
the right or when you turn to the left.
—Isaiah 30:21 ESV

Have you ever felt yourself going off the path God intended you take? Whether due to a busy life, lack of trust, or outright disobedience, getting off God's path poses real danger. Today's date is simple, fun, and adventurous! You and Jesus are going for an evening walk. And while on that walk, I want you to ask Him about the immaculate plans He has for your life.

As He rolls out the blueprint, ask Him what route you need to take to get there and who's coming with you. Lastly, remember that when situations arise that cause you to veer off course, "your ears shall hear a word behind you, saying, 'This is the way, walk in it.'"

— Ask Him —

- What plans do you have for my life?
- What do I need to do to get there?
- Who's coming with me?

Date 4

Scripture Scramble

Your word is a lamp to my feet and a light to my path.
—Psalm 119:105 ESV

Today's date will be fun and quick. I want you to pick three of your favorite scriptures and read them aloud.

Ask Jesus why those three scriptures minister to your heart so deeply.

Take His response, jot it on a sticky note, and put it somewhere that will be visible to you for the next thirty days.

Continue to read the verses aloud and meditate on His responses.

— Tell Him —

- Your thoughts on His responses.

4

Date 5

Date Night, Party of Two!

Lord, I have chosen you alone as my inheritance. You are my prize, my pleasure, and my portion. I leave my destiny and its timing in your hands.
—Psalm 16:5 TPT

Everyone loves date night. It's a time to get all dressed up and hang out with your family, friends, or significant other. Tonight you will cook a meal or grab takeout, then sit down at your dining table, leaving the seat across from you empty.

This date will require you to stretch your imagination and embrace vulnerability. The purpose of this date is for you and Jesus to get to know each other in a deeper way. You might be saying to yourself, "But He knows me, He created me, He knows my thoughts before they enter my mind." While this is true, He doesn't just want to know these things because He's all knowing and all powerful. He wants to know things because His close friend (you) chooses to share them with Him.

Ask Him safe questions, easy questions, hard questions, and crazy questions. He stepped down from His throne

5

to have dinner with you. Don't waste one second of your time together.

— Ask Him —

- How was your day?
- What makes you laugh?
- What are you most proud of?
- What breaks your heart?
- What word would you use to describe me?
- In what areas have I shown tremendous growth over the years?

Weekend

Date 6

Happy Hiking

It is the glory of God to conceal a matter; to
search out a matter is the glory of kings.
—Proverbs 25:2

Sometimes getting out of our normal environment and into the wonder of nature helps to clear our minds and rejuvenate our spirits.

Today, you and Jesus are going for a hike in nature. Enjoy the birds chirping, endless greenery, and the radiant beauty of all of He created.

– Tell Him –

- What you loved most about your walk together.

Weekend

Date 7

Magical Memories at the Museum

The LORD is my strength and shield. I trust him with all my heart. He helps me, and my heart is filled with joy. I burst out in songs of thanksgiving.
—Psalm 28:7 NLT

Museums give us a deeper look at different eras and at priceless artifacts, and they pull us into the movements in history that have shaped our lives. Today you and Jesus are going on an adventure to the museum. You might choose any museum in your area that piques your interest. Take your time walking through and reading why each item holds value and was chosen as an exhibit. Allow Jesus to speak to you through each piece.

— Ask Him —

- What did you enjoy most about our museum date?

Date 8

Purposeful Prayers

Whatever you ask for in prayer, believe that
you have received it, and it will be yours.
—Matthew 11:24

Prayer is a significant part of our Christian walk. It is our lifeline. For today's date, you're going to spend fifteen minutes in prayer. It is important to remove every possible distraction for your purposeful prayer time with Jesus. What you pray about is completely up to you. When your fifteen minutes is up,

— Ask Him —

- What were you doing in those fifteen minutes that I didn't see?

Date 9

Movie Night

Greater love has no one than this: to lay down
one's life for one's friends.
—John 15:13

Tonight you're going to grab your favorite snack and a cozy blanket and snuggle up on the couch with Jesus for a movie night. You will pick a movie from the ten options listed below and then ask Jesus the following questions when it ends. Try to engage your heart in the movie and insert yourself into the plot. Jesus is going to reveal so much to you through this time. Trust me, you'll never want to have another movie night without Him!

— Ask Him —

- What are you doing in my life right now?
- How are my life and this movie connected?

MOVIE OPTIONS

- The Shack
- McFarland, USA
- I Can Only Imagine
- Breakthrough
- Remembering the Titans
- Miracles from Heaven
- Overcomer
- The Blind Side
- God's Not Dead
- I Still Believe

Date 10

Letters of Love

The Lord is my best friend and my shepherd. I always have more than enough.
—Psalms 23:1 TPT

Today's date will be fun and quick! For every letter in your first name, you're going to ask Jesus to give you one word for each letter that describes you! For example, if your name was Ann, you'd ask Him what the A stands for, then the N, and so on, until you complete every letter.

Take a few minutes to research each word's definition. Then do the same for J-E-S-U-S.

— Tell Him —

- What you think of His answers.

Date 11

Puzzled to Pieces

*Trust in the LORD with all your heart and lean
not on your own understanding.*
—*Proverbs 3:5*

Putting together a puzzle requires patience and perseverance. Today you and Jesus are going to intently work together to connect the pieces of a puzzle.

Whether it comes with a thousand pieces or twenty-five
pieces, take your time and allow Him to help you
through it. When you get stuck, ask Him for guidance;
when you get it right, celebrate with Him.

— Ask Him —

- What pieces of my life are you putting back together?

Date 12

Cooking with the King

Abide in me, and I in you. As the branch cannot bear fruit by itself, unless it abides in the vine, neither can you, unless you abide in me.
—John 15:4 ESV

Today you and Jesus are going to have a cooking date. You can make an extravagant peanut butter and jelly sandwich or a three-course meal. What you choose to cook is solely up to you.

The point of today's date is for you to learn how to abide in Him no matter what tasks you're achieving throughout your day. Dating Jesus is less about casual moments together and more about learning how to abide in Him every second of every day. Abiding in Him means being constantly aware of His love and presence, and dwelling and resting in or with Him continuously.

— Ask Him —

- What can I do on a daily basis to abide in you?

Weekend
Date 13

Three's a Crowd

*Where two or three gather in my name, there
am I with them.*
—Matthew 18:20

We can't underestimate the power and value of fellowship. Jesus didn't do life alone. Instead, He chose twelve powerful, influential men to do life with. An old African proverb says "If you want to go fast, go alone. If you want to go far, go together." If you're going to achieve every goal you've set for yourself, you're going to need to be surrounded by a strong team.

Today your date with Jesus will require you to bring along a friend. Choose someone you trust, admire, and love. The three of you can go for coffee, a walk, catch a movie, or just have a much-needed phone conversation.

Share your heart, goals, and plans with them. Lastly, share what Jesus has been showing you through your courtship.

— Ask Him —

- Jesus, what friends have you placed in my life and why?

Weekend

Date 14

Beautiful Sunsets

From the rising of the sun to its setting, the
name of the Lord is to be praised!
—Psalm 113:3 ESV

There is something so magical encompassed in the setting of the sun and its vibrant array of colors intentionally painted onto the canvas of the sky. Today you're going to simply sit with Jesus and watch the sunset.

You might put on worship music or sit in silence. Try to immerse yourself in the moment, ignoring distractions and embracing vulnerability. Allow the mixture of colors and feeling of serenity to replenish the weary places in your heart.

— Tell Him —

- How you feel when you absorb the beauty and peace of His creation.

Date 15

You, YouTube, and Jesus!

Do not be afraid or discouraged, for the LORD
will personally go ahead of you. He will be with
you; he will neither fail you nor abandon you.
—Deuteronomy 31:8 NLT

Today you and Jesus are going to binge watch YouTube! The catch is, whatever you choose to watch must bring nourishment, encouragement, insight, and understanding to your spirit. Whether you choose a TED Talk or a sermon, allow God to minister to your heart and release you from bad habits, character flaws, self-sabotage, and generational bondage.

There will be a moment during your date together today when you'll feel Him pulling on your heart strongly. Yield to His presence and allow Him in.

— Ask Him —

- What load have I been carrying that I was never meant to bear?

Date 16

WILD CARD DATE!

*May he grant your heart's desires and make all
your plans succeed.*
—Psalm 20:4 NLT

A wild card date means that you and Jesus get to choose together what you do today! You can take a stroll through the park, pray together, write a song, go grocery shopping, or grab coffee. You have two requirements: 1) Make it fun, 2) Make it memorable!

— Ask Him —

- Jesus, what did you enjoy most about our spontaneous wild card date?

Date 17

The Ultimate Dance Party!

David danced before the LORD with all his might.
—2 Samuel 6:14 KJV

David is a character in the Bible vastly known for his illustrious dance moves. He would dance before the Lord with all his might. He didn't care how foolish he looked to those around him. His only objective was to glorify the One who had chosen him, loved him, protected him, and blessed him.

Today you're going to tap into your inner David. Put on your favorite worship tunes, clear a space in your home, and dance before the Lord with all your might. As you dance, He is going to break off the chains of performance, fear of people's opinions, shame, guilt, depression, anxiety, and whatever else has been trying to hold you captive. It's time you danced to the beat of your own drum!

— Ask Him —

- What His favorite thing is about dancing.

Date 18

Cookies and Milk!

I am the good shepherd. The good shepherd
sacrifices his life for the sheep.
—John 10:11 NLT

As a child, nothing made me happier than smelling the sweet aroma of my mom's homemade chocolate chip cookies baking. Once they had cooled down, my siblings and I would sit down at the table and enjoy them with a glass of milk. Today you and Jesus are going to enjoy a few of your favorite cookies with a glass of milk (Yes, almond milk is acceptable for those who don't do dairy).

While enjoying your sweet treat, you're going to ask Jesus some questions. I want to encourage you to become vulnerable and open to His responses that might be tough or uncomfortable to hear. Remember that He's there to love and cover you, not ridicule and condemn you. Breathe and trust Him.

— Ask Him —

- What Goliath have I refused to face?
- Do I tend to self-sabotage, and why?
- What areas of my life have I kept you out of?
- What would you like me to release to you?

Date 19

Blessed Be the Birds

*Look at the birds of the air; they do not sow or
reap or store away in barns, and yet your
heavenly Father feeds them. Are you not much
more valuable than they?*
—Matthew 6:26

I love today's scripture because it really puts in perspective how important we are to Jesus. Grasping the revelation of just how much Jesus loves and cares for us has completely changed my life.

Today you and Jesus are going to feed the birds at a nearby park and reflect on your life. Grab some bread, a handy journal, and head out. While there, find a nice place to sit and spend some time reflecting with Jesus. Share with Him things that have disappointed you, dreams you've seen fulfilled, and what you need most from Him. Before you leave, take a few minutes to feed the birds and ponder today's scripture.

— Prayer —

Jesus, thank you for providing for me, always. Thank you for consistently being a soft place for my heart to land. May I continue to recognize the depth of your unfailing love toward me. Amen.

Weekend

Date 20

Let's Walk on Water!

'Come,' he said. Then Peter got down out of the boat, walked on the water and came toward Jesus.
—Matthew 14:29

Today's date will allow you to channel your inner Peter. Yes, you too are about to walk on (frozen) water with Jesus. Though there won't be ferocious winds challenging your faith, this will still be a transformative experience.

Read Matthew 14:22–33. Once finished, head over to the nearest outdoor or indoor ice-skating rink in your area. As you dance with Jesus on the water:

— Ask Him —

- Why did Peter feel safe to come when he heard Jesus beckon him?
- To take you back to that historical moment and share with you the intimate places of His heart.

Weekend

Date 21

I Scream for Ice Cream!

I am leaving you with a gift—peace of mind and heart. And the peace I give is a gift the world cannot give. So don't be troubled or afraid.
—John 14:27 NLT

Today you and Jesus are going on an ice cream date! My dad took me and my siblings for ice cream on Sundays after church. It was always the highlight of my week.

I believe there is something profoundly peaceful about sharing a delightful treat with a Father, confidant, and friend. So head over to your favorite local ice cream shop and order your favorite frozen treat. As you and Jesus spend this time together:

— Ask Him —

- What childhood misconceptions about myself would you like to repair during our ice cream date?

Date 22

Coloring Date

*I praise you because I am fearfully and
wonderfully made; your works are wonderful, I
know that full well.*
—Psalm 139:14

When's the last time you grabbed a coloring book and
challenged your third grade coloring skills? For today's
date, you're going to need a good coloring book and a
pack of crayons (you can get both from the Dollar Store).
Flip through the book until you find a page that jumps
out at you. Once you have it, begin coloring. As you
choose your colors and start creating your masterpiece,

— Ask Him —

- How He created you.
- How He chose the colors.
- What about you most reflects Him.

Date 23

Flower-Picking Party

As for man, his days are like grass; he
flourishes like a flower of the field.
—*Psalm 103:15 ESV*

When's the last time you went and picked flowers? I don't mean picked up flowers from your local grocery store but actually went to a field and created your own quirky, unique bouquet? Well, today you and Jesus are going on a flower-picking date! Find a nearby field or another place full of wildflowers. Once there, you and Him will create a bouquet of flowers unique to you.

— Ask Him —

- Why He chose certain flowers for you.
- Why the colors are significant.

Date 24

Hey, Future Me, Part 1

We know and rely on the love God has for us.
God is love. Whoever lives in love lives in God,
and God in them.
—1 John 4:16

Today you're going to sit down with Jesus and write a letter to your future self. Ask Jesus what your future self will need to hear when you go back to reread this letter later in the book. Allow Him to guide your hand and give you specific scriptures and words of encouragement. Once you're done, sign off with your name and today's date and time. Keep your letter in a safe place until you get to date 75, when you'll reread it.

— Ask Him —

- What will I need to hear later?

Date 25

Bookworm

Then I said, 'Behold, I have come—
In the volume of the book it is written of Me—
To do Your will, O God.'
—Hebrews 10:7 NKJV

One of the best ways to spend time with Jesus is to read the inspirational words of the Bible. Today you're going to sit down and read through the Bible with Jesus. You might choose any book, verse, or chapter out of the four Gospels (Matthew, Mark, Luke, John). These four books encompass the remarkable life of Jesus. They share His highs, lows, miracles, and unfailing love. As you read, open your heart to Him and surrender your imagination to the moment. Allow Him to bring you into the stories you're reading.

— Ask Him —

- What new revelation would you like to give me from today's reading?

Date 26

Declutter Lover

*A time to search and a time to give up, a time
to keep and a time to throw away.*
—Ecclesiastes 3:6

There is nothing quite like purging your closet of items you won't wear, don't wear, and haven't worn in years. We all have that shirt, dress, sweater, or cardigan that hasn't seen daylight since the day we bought it.

When we remove things from our lives that no longer serve us, we open up a space for Jesus to give us the things that will. Today you two will be decluttering your closet.

As you look over items and reminisce, ask Him what items you should get rid of. Carefully remove the items and bag them up. A later date will give you the next steps. Be open, and be prepared to get rid of things you might still like. Most importantly, have fun!

— Ask Him —

- What items should I get rid of?

Weekend

Date 27

Hanging at the Zoo!

God said, 'Let the earth bring forth living
creatures according to their kinds—livestock
and creeping things and beasts of the earth
according to their kinds.' And it was so.
—Genesis 1:24 ESV

Today you and Jesus are going on a date to the zoo! Yep, you heard me correctly; you're going to party hardy at the zoo with Jesus. Today's date will be casual, informative, possibly smelly, and fun!

As you walk through the zoo with Jesus, ask Him to share with you what it was like on day six of creation when He created the animals.

Feel free to put your earbuds in and listen to some worship music while you stroll through. Spend some time with the animals; watch them interact, sleep, eat, and play. Today, Jesus plans to reveal another side of His heart to you. :)

— Ask Him —

- What was creating the animal kingdom like?

Weekend

Date 28

Blissful Bike Rides

"In him we live and move and have our being."
As some of your own poets have said, "We are
his offspring."
—Acts 17:28

Today you and Jesus are going for a bike ride. Try to pick a nice trail surrounded by nature's bliss. As you ride through the trees admiring the wonder of His creation, ask Him this question:

— Ask Him —

- What was I created for?

Date 29

The Gift of Giving

*In everything I did, I showed you that by this
kind of hard work we must help the weak,
remembering the words the Lord Jesus himself
said: 'It is more blessed to give than to receive.'*
—*Acts 20:35*

A few days ago, you and Jesus spent some time decluttering your closet. Today you're going to take all of the items you bagged up to your nearest secondhand store.

As you give those items away, remember Jesus's words "It is more blessed to give than to receive" (Acts 20:35). With every item given, Jesus is going to give you something in return. Maybe He's giving you peace, perspective, increased wisdom, restoration, or more ammo to annihilate your enemy, Satan. As you head back home, I want you to ask Jesus this question:

— Ask Him —

- What did you give me in return?

Date 30

Picnics and Prayers

The faithful love of the LORD never ends! His mercies never cease.
—Lamentations 3:22 NLT

Life needs a few more polka dots and picnics. —Unknown

I couldn't agree more with this quote. Today you and Jesus are going on a picnic date! While together, I want you to spend some time in prayer. When I say prayer, I simply mean a time of intimate conversation with Jesus. Talk to Him about your desires. Most importantly, spend time *thanking Him* for all He's done. Prayer is our cordless phone to heaven, so make the most of this call!

— Ask Him —

- What does my future look like?
- What should I be focusing on?

PICNIC CHECKLIST

- Bible
- Journal
- Blanket
- Basket or canvas bag
- Cooler
- Chair (if you don't want to sit on the ground)
- Food
- Drinks
- Utensils, plates, cups, napkins

Date 31

WILD CARD DATE!

Now all glory to God, who is able, through his mighty power at work within us, to accomplish infinitely more than we might ask or think.
—Ephesians 3:20 NLT

A wild card date means that you and Jesus get to choose together what you do today! You can take a stroll through the park, watch a movie, make dinner, or grab coffee. You have two requirements:

1) Make it fun.

2) Make it memorable!

— Ask Him —

- Jesus, what did you enjoy most about our spontaneous wild card date?

Date 32

Mirror, Mirror on the Wall

God created mankind in his own image, in the image of God he created them; male and female he created them.
—Genesis 1:27

Positive affirmations help to reprogram our thought patterns. When we constantly repeat positive affirmations, we create positive subconscious thoughts. This helps to keep our heart, mind, and soul healthy.

Today you and Jesus are going to create ten positive affirmations together. Take ten sticky notes into your bathroom, look in the mirror, and ask Jesus what He says about you. Write down one thing on each sticky note.

Then for the next twenty-one days, recite His words over yourself and watch everything begin to change.

— Ask Him —

- What do you say about me?

Date 33

Podcasts and Perspective

The beginning of wisdom is this: Get wisdom.
Though it cost all you have, get understanding.
—Proverbs 4:7

Today you and Jesus are going to listen to an educational podcast. Podcasts are a great way to stay mentally, spiritually, and emotionally nourished while managing a busy life.

Ask Jesus what area you need more understanding in, type it in the search bar with the word "podcast," and pick a title that interests you.

As you listen to your chosen podcast, allow Jesus to give you new perspective and deeper wisdom on things.

— Ask Him —

- What area do I need more understanding in?

Weekend

Date 34

Bowling Alleys and Breakthroughs

*When the people heard the sound of the rams'
horns, they shouted as loud as they could.
Suddenly, the walls of Jericho collapsed, and
the Israelites charged straight into the town
and captured it.*
—Joshua 6:20 NLT

Today you and Jesus are going on a fun date to the bowling alley. Before you head out, take a second to read the infamous Bible story about the walls of Jericho coming down (Joshua 6). This story takes us on the Israelites' journey to victory and breakthrough. After you read the story, head to a bowling alley in your area. There, Jesus will begin to show you what walls He wants to break down in your life and where He wants to bring breakthrough.

— Ask Him —

- What walls in my life are you breaking down?

Weekend

Date 35

Pottery Class

Yet you, LORD, are our Father. We are the clay, you are the potter; we are all the work of your hand.
— Isaiah 64:8

Today you and Jesus are going to take a pottery class together. As you sit and mold the clay, allow Him to guide your hands and share with you what it's like to be the potter of the world! Really lean into His heart and allow His words to shape and mold the way you've seen life.

— Ask Him —

- What's it like to shape the world?

Date 36

Naps with Jesus

*"Come to me, all of you who are weary and
carry heavy burdens, and I will give you rest."*
—Acts 17:28 NLT

Maybe you're saying, "I thought this book was supposed to deepen my relationship with Jesus, not with my bed." The thing is, rest is a prime way for us to enter into the loving arms of Jesus and be rejuvenated, refreshed, and refilled, and napping says "I trust you enough to rest my body, mind, and spirit. I know that you're taking care of things while also refilling my cup." So say the prayer below and go take a nap!

Prayer

Jesus, teach me how to rest more in you. Teach me how to shut off my mind, slow down, and enter into your blissful rest. I trust that you can do more when I rest than I can do in a lifetime. Watch over me, give me dreams, and allow me to wake up feeling rejuvenated. I'm thankful for every moment we share together. Amen

— Ask Him —

- What kind of rest do you recommend for me?

Date 37

Rip the Runway

Blessed is the one who trusts in the LORD,
whose confidence is in him.
—Jeremiah 17:7

Imagine yourself on a long runway, hair blowing in the wind, cameras flashing, and crowds of people cheering your name. You're walking with unquenchable confidence, knowing that it's your time, your moment; and all eyes are focused on you. Your date today with Jesus will encompass all of this.

Rummage through your closet and pick out a fun outfit, put on your ceiling fan, prop up your phone, put on the flash, play your favorite song, find a hallway in your home, and let Jesus cheer you on as you confidently rip the runway! The purpose of this date is to allow Jesus to ignite your confidence. Everything changes when you know you're being cheered for and seen by the One who loves you most.

— Ask Him —

- When's the last time you were cheering me on?

Date 38

Sidewalk and Chalk

*Truly, I say to you, unless you turn and
become like children, you will never enter the
kingdom of heaven.*
—Matthew 18:3 ESV

Do you ever reminisce on the days when you'd draw beautiful masterpieces on the sidewalk with chalk? You felt like a natural-born Leonardo da Vinci. Today you and Jesus are going to relive your sidewalk and chalk glory days. You're going to draw three pictures together on the sidewalk.

You might involve your spouse, children, friends, family, and neighbors in this date if you'd like. The purpose of today's date is to tap into your childlike self, have fun, let down your hair, and create something magical with Jesus. You'll choose the first drawing, He'll choose the second, and together you'll choose the third. Be open to branching out of your comfort zone during this date.

— Ask Him —

- What did you enjoy most about our date today?

Date 39

Canvas of Love

He has made everything beautiful in its time.
He has also set eternity in the human heart; yet
no one can fathom what God has done from
beginning to end.
—Ecclesiastes 3:11

Today, your date with Jesus will require you to tap into your creative side. I'm not asking you to turn into Picasso but I am asking you to give this date a fair shot, no matter your artistic level. Here is what you'll need: a blank canvas, a few paintbrushes, and some paint. Great news—you can grab all of these items at your nearest Dollar Store. Once home, set everything up and begin painting a picture of you and Jesus together. There is no right or wrong way to illustrate you and Jesus. Allow your imagination to flow and, most importantly, have *fun!*

— Share Them —

Please email your pictures to stephaniealexisauthor@gmail.com. Or hashtag #100dateswithjesus on Instagram or Facebook. I would love to see them.

Date 40

To Worship You, I Live

Let everything that has breath praise the LORD!
Hallelujah!
—Psalm 150:6 NASB

Worship is a way to show Jesus how much we love, honor, and need Him. It is what we were created for. When we surrender our hearts in worship, we get Jesus's attention. Today I want you to take some time to just worship Him. This might look like singing along to a playlist of songs or dancing before Him. Whatever your heart longs to do, do that. There is no formula for worship. Surrender everything to Him in this moment!

— Ask Him —

- What happens when I meet you in worship?

Weekend

Date 41

Volunteer with Cheer

*God is not unjust; he will not forget your work
and the love you have shown him as you have
helped his people and continue to help them.*
—*Hebrews 6:10*

Today you and Jesus are going to volunteer together. You might pick to serve at your church, a homeless shelter, animal shelter, food bank, the Boys and Girls Club, or anywhere you two choose. It's important that you choose together. Jesus will help direct you to a place where your expertise, heart, and time are most needed. Once you finish, reflect on what you enjoyed most about serving today.

— Ask Him —

- What did I bring to that environment that was needed?

Weekend

Date 42

Aquarium Adventures

God created the great sea creatures and every
living creature that moves, with which the
waters swarm, according to their kinds, and
every winged bird according to its kind. And
God saw that it was good.
—Genesis 1:21 ESV

Today you and Jesus are going on a date to the aquarium! You'll be greeted by beautiful seahorses, colorful fish, snakes, frogs, and other amphibians. As you walk through the aquarium with Jesus, google fun facts about your favorite aquatic animals. Feel free to put your earbuds in and listen to some worship music while you stroll through. Spend some time with the animals and watch them interact, sleep, eat, and play. Tell Him what you enjoyed most about today's date!

— Ask Him —

- What did you enjoy most about today's date?

Date 43

Window-Shopping

*Delight yourself in the LORD, and he will give
you the desires of your heart.*
—Psalm 37:4 ESV

Window-shopping is a favorite hobby of mine. I like to window-shop at the mall or online, but my favorite is window-shopping beautiful homes in grand neighborhoods.

When most people quote today's scripture, their desires are usually for materialistic items. "Oh, if I delight myself in Him, I'll get that new job," "Oh, if I delight myself in Him, I'll get that new car or house." Though Jesus might grant these requests, I don't believe they are at the very top of His list of desires to fulfill.

When we allow Jesus to go deep into our hearts and heal our trauma, our desires begin to change. We go from wanting what we want to wanting what He wants for us. Today you're going to pick a place, any place, to do some window-shopping with Jesus. As you walk around and browse, ask Him:

— Ask Him —

- Are my desires aligning with your desires?
- What would you like to heal in my heart?

Date 44

Apple Picking!

My flesh and my heart may fail, but God is the strength of my heart and my portion forever.
—Psalm 73:26 ESV

Have you ever gone apple picking? If your answer is no, then you get to have your first apple-picking experience with Jesus. Find an orchard nearby and go have some fun. As the two of you observe the apples and pick the ones you believe to be the best, talk to Him about some of the areas you've been struggling in lately.

— Ask Him —

- What is your wisdom and advice on how to become unstuck?

Date 45

Trying a New Restaurant

*God will do this, for he is faithful to do what he
says, and he has invited you into partnership
with his Son, Jesus Christ our Lord.*
—*1 Corinthians 1:9 NLT*

Today you and Jesus are going to try a new restaurant together! You might choose to go for breakfast, lunch, or dinner. Feel free to bring your earbuds to listen to worship music, a journal to write down your thoughts, or your Bible. The point of today's date is to experience new things and create new memories with Jesus.

— Ask Him —

- What new thing are you doing in my life?

Date 46

Baking Bread with the Bread of Life

Jesus replied, "I am the bread of life. Whoever
comes to me will never be hungry again.
Whoever believes in me will never be thirsty."
—*John 6:35 NLT*

After Jesus fed the five thousand, not counting the women and children (John 6), He revealed to them that He was, in fact, the *Bread of Life,* and that whoever comes to Him will never be hungry again. Today you and Jesus are going to do something you might have never done—make bread!

Don't worry, I've included a very simple recipe to help guide you along. As you make bread with the Bread of Life, listen to or read John 6 and ask Jesus to take you deeper into that passage of Scripture. Allow Him to take over your imagination and really take you into this sacred moment.

Prayer

Thank you for being the Bread of Life. Thank you for giving me life and sacrificing yourself for me. May we create a lifelong romance where I'm permitted to know the deep things of your heart. May I see you as the righteous King you are, viewing your story through lenses untainted. May I love you unconditionally, just as you have loved me.

— *Ask Him* —

- Tell me more about how you are the Bread of Life.

BREAD RECIPE

· 1 cup all-purpose flour

· $\frac{1}{3}$ cup vegetable oil or olive oil

· $\frac{1}{8}$ teaspoon salt

· $\frac{1}{3}$ cup water

Instructions:

1. Preheat oven to 425 degrees F (220 degrees C). Line a baking sheet with parchment paper.
2. Mix flour, oil, and salt together in a bowl; add water and mix using a pastry cutter until dough is soft. Form dough into 6 balls and press into disks onto the prepared baking sheet using your hands.
3. Bake in the preheated oven until bread is cooked, 8 to 10 minutes.
4. Cool, brush with butter and enjoy!

Date 47

Self-Care Is for Everyone

God is within her, she will not fall; God will
help her at break of day.
—Psalm 46:5

Did you know that Jesus cares about your self-care routine? I mean, really, really, really cares about it? Well, He does. It's not His will for us to live life constantly burned out, impaired, fatigued, and hopeless.

Today your date with Jesus will be centered all around doing something that will rejuvenate your mind, bring peace to your spirit, and bless your soul. Below you'll find a list of self-care ideas. Ask Jesus which three activities He wants you to do, then complete them. Once finished, ask Him:

— Ask Him —

- Why did you choose those specific activities for me?

SELF-CARE IDEAS

· Get a pedicure or a manicure

· Take a nap

· Turn off your phone

· Drink water

· Order takeout

· Exercise

· Dance to your favorite song

· Read a book or magazine for an hour

· Do something crafty: coloring, knitting, sewing

· Sit in the grass and watch the clouds float by

· Burn a candle or diffuse some oils

· Go for a drive

· Take a bubble bath

· Go to bed early or sleep in late

· Declutter a spot in your house

· Get a massage

· Write a list of ten things you're grateful for

· Cook a fancy meal for no other reason than you deserve a fancy meal

· Say no to someone

· Take a hot shower

· Plant something

· Donate your time

· Listen to a podcast

· Eat breakfast

· Laugh with friends

· Plan a small getaway

· Take a course in something new

· Grab your favorite coffee

· Wash your hair

· Watch a movie

· Make your bed

· Take a social media break

· Do nothing

· Catch up on your favorite show

· Learn the basics of a new language

Weekend

Date 48

Local Sporting Event

Everyone who competes in the games goes into strict training. They do it to get a crown that will not last, but we do it to get a crown that will last forever.
—1 Corinthians 9:25

Today you and Jesus are going to a local sporting event. You can check out a high school football game, ballet recital, baseball game, bowling competition, or any other sporting activity you'd like. While there, pick a team to root for and cheer them on to victory.

— Ask Him —

- What are you training me for?

Weekend

Date 49

Beach Bound

When you pass through the waters, I will be
with you; and when you pass through the
rivers, they will not sweep over you.
—Isaiah 43:2

Water is symbolic of many things—baptism, cleansing, purifying, and lots more. Jesus refers to Himself, among other things, as living water (John 4:10).

Today, you and Jesus are going to spend some quality time together at the beach, pond, or lake—whether you just put your toes in, immerse your whole body, or just sit in your car and watch the water.

Allow yourself to be fully aware of His peaceful presence. If possible, listen to "Oceans (where feet may fail)" by Hillsong United.

— Ask Him —

- Speak to me about your living water.

Date 50

Communion

When He had given thanks, He broke it and said, 'This is My body, which is for you; do this in remembrance of Me.' In the same way He took the cup also after supper, saying, 'This cup is the new covenant in My blood; do this, as often as you drink it, in remembrance of Me.' For as often as you eat this bread and drink the cup, you proclaim the Lord's death until He comes.'
—1 Corinthians 11:24 NASB

Growing up, I only thought you were permitted to do communion on special occasions, but as I grew older, I discovered the value, power, and sanctification in doing communion often. Whether that's once a month or once a week, there is an intimacy and purifying that happens when we consume the body (bread) and blood (wine) of Jesus in remembrance of Him.

Today you and Jesus are going to take communion to-gether. Please don't be discouraged if you don't have the "proper" food items for this. I once heard of a woman do-ing communion at an AA meeting and all they had was a bottle of Coke and cough drops. Needless to say, many gave their life to Christ that day.

Grab a piece of bread, a cracker, a pretzel, or whatever you have at home to represent His body. Then pour a little wine, grape juice, cranberry juice, or whatever you have in your fridge that can represent His blood. It is less about what you use and more about your heart to honor Him.

Instructions

- Read over today's scripture one more time.

- Take your bread (or whatever you're using to represent His body), hold it up to Jesus, and say "This is your body, which was broken for me; I take this in remembrance of you."

- Take your wine (or whatever you're using to represent His blood), hold it up to Jesus, and say "This cup represents the new covenant in your blood; I drink this in remembrance of you."

Prayer

May your body and your blood purify my heart, cleanse my mind, realign my body, and restore my soul. May I never forget the sacrifice you made for me. Amen.

— Ask Him —

- How can I commune with you more often?

Date 51

Self-Reflection and Direction

*I am the vine; you are the branches. If you
remain in me and I in you, you will bear much
fruit; apart from me you can do nothing.*
—John 15:5

True connection doesn't come without self-reflection. Dating Jesus is awesome, but really being connected to Him, bearing sustainable fruit obtained from the vine, is priceless. Today you and Jesus are going to do some deep self-reflection. Grab your Bible, grab your journal, head to your prayer closet, put on some soaking music, and lean into His presence.

— Ask Him —

- Is there anything in me that doesn't reflect you?
- Where have I shown growth over the years?
- Is there any part of my life where I've put distance between us?
- Are there any idols in my life?

Date 52

Dancing Down Memory Lane

Teach these new disciples to obey all the commands I have given you. And be sure of this: I am with you always, even to the end of the age.
—*Matthew 28:20 NLT*

Today, you and Jesus are going to take a fun trip down memory lane. If you have an old photo album, go grab it, or jump on one of your social media platforms. Find a cozy place to sit with your favorite snack and browse through your pictures. Talk to Jesus about what you remember from each day. Allow each memory to come alive in your mind. Pick one memory that brings you joy and ask Jesus the question below.

— Ask Him —

- Where were you in this memory?

Date 53

Bible Trivia

How much better to get wisdom than gold, to
get insight rather than silver!
—Proverbs 16:16

Everyone loves a good game of trivia! Today you and Jesus are going to do some fun Bible trivia. Well, you'll mainly be the one being quizzed since He lived it.

Below you'll find some fun questions that will test your knowledge of the New and Old Testament. You'll find the answers to each question at the back of the book. I encourage you to really dig deep and test your Bible knowledge. (Use the answer guide at the back of the book as your last resort.)

— Trivia Questions —

1. In what city was Jesus born?

2. How many books are in the Old Testament?

3. How many days did God take to create the world?

4. Who was the first man?

5. Who was the first woman?

6. How many days and nights did it rain when Noah was on the ark?

7. What was God's sign to Noah that he would never destroy the earth again?

8. How many brothers did Joseph have?

9. What did Jacob give Joseph that sparked jealousy from his siblings?

10. How did Moses's mother save him from the Egyptian soldiers?

11. Through what did God speak to Moses in the desert?

12. How many plagues did God send on Egypt?

13. When Pharaoh changed his mind and sent his army after the slaves, where did they meet?

14. Where did God give Moses the Ten Commandments?

15. Who was the first king of Israel?

16. When Daniel prayed to God after it was not allowed, what was he thrown into?

17. Who was Jesus's mother?

18. Who baptized Jesus?

19. Before Jesus started preaching, what was His job?

20. Name Jesus's hometown.

21. Name the place where Jesus walked on water?

22. How many disciples did Jesus choose?

23. What is the shortest verse in the Bible?

24. Why did Jesus cry in that verse?

25. How much bread and fish did Jesus use to feed more than five thousand people?

26. What did Jesus do at the Last Supper to His disciples?

27. What did the woman pour on Jesus's feet at the home of Simon, the man with leprosy?

28. Name the disciple who betrayed Jesus.

29. Which disciple denied Jesus three times?

30. What does Jesus say is the first and greatest commandment?

— Ask Him —

- What question would you like to ask me?

Date 54

Creating a Budget

You shall remember the LORD your God, for it is he who gives you power to get wealth, that he may confirm his covenant that he swore to your fathers, as it is this day.
—Deuteronomy 8:18 ESV

I know you're probably thinking that a budgeting date doesn't sound like the most exciting date on the planet. Though it might not make you want to jump for joy, it is a big part of Jesus's plan for your life. Throughout the Bible, we're given many important principles on how to handle money and finances.

A budget is nothing more than a plan for saving and spending money. A good budget takes care of all the regular and important bills—like rent or mortgage, utilities, food, gasoline, and insurance—and allows for the unexpected or occasional expenses. Jesus wants you to have control over your finances, and budgeting can be a helpful and wise tool. Below you will see an example of things you might want to include in your budget.

BUDGET

- Mortgage/rent
- Homeowner's or renter's insurance
- Property tax (if not already included in the mortgage payment)
- Auto insurance
- Health insurance
- Out-of-pocket medical costs
- Life insurance
- Electricity and natural gas
- Water
- Sanitation/garbage
- Groceries, toiletries, and other essentials
- Car payment
- Gasoline
- Public transportation
- Personal care
- Eating out
- Internet
- Cell phone and/or landline
- Student loan payments
- Entertainment
- Savings
- Travel
- Other minimum loan payments
- Child support or alimony payments
- Childcare

Jesus, I thank you for everything you have allowed me to be a steward over. I break off any unhealthy ties, ideas, concepts, and mentalities I've acquired over the years toward money. I declare that all of my needs are met because you are my provider. I ask that you would help me to create a budget that will work for me. Allow me to be honest with myself regarding my spending. I invite you into my finances. Teach me how to manage my spending and my savings. Amen.

- Who would you like me to give to next?

Weekend

Date 55

Donating Red Love

He is so rich in kindness and grace that he
purchased our freedom with the blood of his
Son and forgave our sins.
—Ephesians 1:7 NLT

Today you and Jesus are going on a date to your local blood center. There, you will donate your blood to support the life of a fellow brother or sister in Christ. Jesus's redemptive blood that was shed on the cross for you has removed your sins and purchased your freedom. As you sit and donate blood today, I want you to ask Jesus what it was like for Him to donate His blood to redeem all of humanity.

Blood Donation Facts from Cedars-Sinai

- One donation can potentially save up to three lives.
- Every two seconds, someone in the United States needs blood.
- 4.5 million Americans will need a blood transfusion each year.

- Red blood cells carry oxygen to the body's organs and tissues.
- The blood type most often requested by hospitals is Type O.
- Blood makes up about seven percent of your body's weight.

Blood donation takes about an hour of your time and could save someone's life.

— Ask Him —

- Why did you think humanity was worth saving?

Weekend

Date 56

Gathering Groceries

If you keep my commandments, you will abide
in my love, just as I have kept my Father's
commandments and abide in his love.
—John 15:10 ESV

Today you and Jesus are going to do a normal weekly activity together—grocery shopping. The point of this date is to get in the habit of including Jesus in every part of your life. You don't just want to spend five minutes with Him when you wake up in the morning and neglect Him for the rest of the day. Instead, you want to learn how to abide in Him, yes? As you walk around the grocery store,

— Ask Him —

- Can you give me some meal ideas?
- Are there any suggestions you have to improve my health!

Date 57

Strolls through the Park

I will answer them before they even call to me.
While they are still talking about their needs, I
will go ahead and answer their prayers!
—Isaiah 65:24 NLT

Today you and Jesus are going to take a stroll through the park together. As you walk, I want you to meditate on today's scripture in the various translations written below. Become more aware of the character of Jesus and of how much He loves you!

Isaiah 65:24, Different Translations

- "Before they call I will answer; while they are still speaking I will hear."

- "Before they even call out to me, I will answer them; before they've finished telling me what they need, I'll have already heard" (TPT).

- "I will answer them before they even call to me. While they are still talking about their needs, I will go ahead and answer their prayers!" (NLT).

- "Even before they call, I will answer, and while they are still speaking, I will hear" (BSB).

- "It shall come to pass. That before they call, I will answer; And while they are still speaking, I will hear" (NKJV).

— *Ask Him* —

- Why do I prefer the (your favorite) translation of your Word?

Date 58

Learning a New Language

Undoubtedly there are all sorts of languages in the world, yet none of them is without meaning.
—1 Corinthians 14:10 NLT

Don't let the title of today's date make you nervous or intimidated. Learning a new language can be fun, rewarding, and exciting.

Today you're going to take on the task of learning a new language with Jesus. Though He speaks every language known to man, this will be a great bonding experience for you both. So what you're going to do first is ask Jesus what language you should learn. Then get on YouTube and type in "learning _____ for beginners."

If you learn three new words, you've done well. Maybe try learning how to pronounce your name in your chosen language, or how to say "Hi, how are you?" This date has two rules: Rule #1 – Keep it simple. Rule #2 – Keep it fun.

– Ask Him –

- Why did you create so many languages?

70

Date 59

Business Brainstorming Party

The LORD your God will bless you as he has promised, and you will lend to many nations but will borrow from none. You will rule over many nations but none will rule over you.
—Deuteronomy 15:6

Do you have a business and are you in need of a supernatural strategy to take it to the next level? Or do you feel called to start a business and need guidance on where to begin and what it's going to look like? If you answered yes to any of those questions, then today's date will be extremely beneficial to you.

Jesus is any smart business owner's first partner. In Deuteronomy, He tells us that the Lord our God will bless us as He has promised and that we will be the lender and not the borrower, and that we will rule over many nations. I want you to grab your favorite go-to beverage, sit down with your journal, and brainstorm with Jesus about your current or future business. Ask Him for new strategies, people you should connect with, and what the future of your business will look like.

Jesus, thank you for being the best business partner I could ever ask for. I ask that you continue to guide me in all knowledge and truth. May my business be a direct reflection of your kingdom. Amen.

— Ask Him —

- What's the next simple thing I should do for my business?

Date 60

Memory Check

*Go, and I will be with your mouth and teach
you what you shall speak.*
—Exodus 4:12 ESV

Today you're going to spend some time with Jesus memorizing scriptures! You might pick the scripture you want to memorize, and I'll also drop a few powerful scripture suggestions below. The point of this date is to sharpen your spiritual tool belt. Sometimes we're faced with challenges that can only be combatted with Scripture. The next time you feel the enemy trying to take territory that doesn't belong to him, you'll be able to quote one of the scriptures you learned today.

— Scripture Suggestions —

2 Corinthians 10:5 We destroy arguments and every lofty opinion raised against the knowledge of God, and take every thought captive to obey Christ.

2 Corinthians 5:17 If anyone is in Christ, he is a new creation. The old has passed away; behold, the new has come.

Hebrews 11:6 He rewards those who seek him.

Isaiah 26:3 You will keep him in perfect peace whose mind is stayed on You, because he trusts in You.

Isaiah 40:31 Those who wait on the LORD shall renew their strength; they shall mount up with wings like eagles, they shall run and not be weary, they shall walk and not faint.

Isaiah 41:10 Fear not, for I am with you; be not dismayed, for I am your God; I will strengthen you, I will help you, I will uphold you with my righteous right hand.

James 4:7 Humble yourselves before God. Resist the devil, and he will flee from you.

Jeremiah 29:11 "I know the plans I have for you," declares the Lord, "plans for welfare and not for evil, to give you a future and a hope."

Proverbs 3:5–6 Trust in the LORD with all your heart, and lean not on your own understanding; in all your ways acknowledge Him, and He shall direct your paths.

Psalm 139:14 I praise you, for I am fearfully and wonderfully made. Wonderful are your works; my soul knows it very well.

Psalms 119:11 Your word I have hidden in my heart, that I might not sin against You!

Psalms 23:1 The Lord is my best friend and my shepherd. I always have more than enough.

Psalms 56:3 Whenever I am afraid, I will trust in You.

— Ask Him —

- What's a new scripture you would like me to memorize?

Date 61

WILD CARD DATE!

He will yet fill your mouth with laughter, and
your lips with shouting.
—John 8:21 ESV

Instructions: A wild card date means that you and Jesus get to choose together what you do today! You can take a jog through the park, grab lunch, write a poem, or grab coffee. You have two requirements: 1) Make it fun. 2) Make it memorable!

– Ask Him –

- Jesus, what did you enjoy most about our spontaneous wild card date?

Weekend

Date 62

Fair Fun

*I recommend having fun, because there is
nothing better for people in this world than to
eat, drink, and enjoy life. That way they will
experience some happiness along with all the
hard work God gives them under the sun.*
—*Ecclesiastes 8:15 NLT*

Today you and Jesus are going on a fun date to the fair. Whether you munch on fried Oreos, ride the Ferris wheel, pet the animals, or create some cool arts and crafts, the point of this date is to learn how to enjoy your most fun, memorable moments with Jesus. He wants to be acknowledged by you. He wants you to be fully aware that no matter where life takes you, He is on the adventure with you.

Tell Him

- What was your favorite part of today's date?

Weekend

Date 63

Church Date

Let the word of Christ dwell in you richly, teaching and admonishing one another in all wisdom, singing psalms and hymns and spiritual songs, with thankfulness in your hearts to God.
—Colossians 3:16 ESV

Corporate worship really moves the heart of Jesus! He loves to see His children together worshiping Him in unity. Today you're going to find a church service to attend with Jesus. While you're there, really allow yourself to be fully present in the moment, in His presence.

— Ask Him —

- What's a good worship song for me to play on repeat right now?

Date 64

Feeling Feelings

Those who sow in tears
Shall reap in joy.
—Psalm 126:5 NKJV

Today you and Jesus are going to have a conversation about how you feel. When I say "how you feel," I don't mean I'm looking for the "I'm great" that you give everyone around you. I want you to tap into how your heart is really doing. Then allow Jesus to bring restoration, clarity, and comfort to the wounded places.

Ask Yourself

- Heart, how are you?

— Ask Him —

- What's next in my healing process?

Date 65

Netflix and Jesus

*The way you live will always honor and please
the Lord, and your lives will produce every
kind of good fruit. All the while, you will grow
as you learn to know God better and better.*
—*Colossians 1:10 NLT*

Everyone loves a good Netflix series, and I've got the perfect one for you to watch with Jesus. You might pick to watch the Gospel of John, the Gospel of Matthew, the Gospel of Mark, or the Gospel of Luke. Each of these captivating movies depicts the life of Jesus from a different perspective.

Try to eliminate distractions and really be present during your Netflix date with Him. Grab a snack and a cold beverage and enjoy this time together.

— Ask Him —

- Which of the four Gospels should I start reading?

Date 66

Breakfast with the Beloved

He says, 'Be still, and know that I am God; I will be exalted among the nations, I will be exalted in the earth.'
—Psalm 46:10

Today you and Jesus are going to enjoy a breakfast date together. Whether you make it or you go out, take the time to really get to know Him deeper on this date. Ask Him questions you've never asked before, and allow Him to take you into the hidden treasures of His heart. He's willing to take you as deep as you want to go!

— Ask Him —

- What treasures have you hidden in my heart?

Date 67

Prophesy His Promise

You can all prophesy in turn so that everyone
may be instructed and encouraged.
—1 Corinthians 14:31

Did you know you have the God-given ability to prophesy? Yep, that's right; you know how to hear from Jesus and release what He is saying. I want to first encourage you by saying that you hear from Jesus very well. You and Him are best friends, and your heart knows when He is speaking.

Today you and Jesus are going to pick five people to prophesy over and encourage by sharing with them what Jesus wants to tell them. This could be a scripture, song, or word. Take a second and ask Jesus who He wants to encourage, and then reach out to them and share what He's saying.

Try not to go into introspection and overthink this! Jesus wants to speak to them, and He wants to use you to do it. Don't limit Him to only speaking one way. Be brave and courageous, precious one.

— Ask Him —

- How does nature tell me when you are speaking?

Date 68

Vision Board Party

The LORD answered me: 'Write the vision;
make it plain on tablets, so he may run who
reads it.'
—Habakkuk 2:2 ESV

A vision board is a collage of images, pictures, and affirmations of a person's dreams and desires. It is designed to serve as a source of inspiration and motivation. Might I add, it's also a really fun arts and crafts project that allows you to see what your goals would look like once you achieve them. So today, you and Jesus are aligning your visions and you're going to put them on a board.

On the next page, you'll see a list of everything you'll need to bring your vision board to life. When you're finished, put it somewhere where you'll be able to see it and reflect on it. It might be a good idea to research other people's vision boards before you start, just to get some inspiration.

— Ask Him —

- How do you use visual clues to inspire me?

MATERIALS

- Poster board
- Magazines
- Other images and text from artwork, old books, computer printouts, etc. (optional)
- Scissors
- Glue sticks
- Paper and pen
- Permanent markers

Weekend

Date 69

Belly Laughs and Popcorn

*He will yet fill your mouth with laughter and
your lips with shouts of joy.*
—Job 8:21

Today you and Jesus are going on a fun date to the movie
theatre! Together, you're going to browse showings at
your local theatre and pick a funny movie from the listing
to entertain you two for next few hours. If possible, try to
leave the seat next to you open and truly allow yourself
to be fully aware that Jesus, the Light of the World, is sit-
ting next to you. Don't forget to grab your popcorn, soda,
and candy. Everyone knows that it's not a memorable
movie date without overly buttery popcorn!

Ask Jesus (and yourself)

- What was your favorite part of our date?
- What was your favorite part of the movie?

Weekend

Date 70

Puppies and Kittens

The godly care for their animals, but the wicked
are always cruel.
—Proverbs 12:10 NLT

Today you and Jesus are going on a date to the animal shelter to look at all the cute, amazing, precious animals that are up for adoption. Research an animal shelter in your area, and call to see when they have availability. Some places will even allow you to play with the animals and take them for a walk. If Jesus leads you to adopt, that's awesome, but it's not a requirement.

As you and Jesus walk through the shelter, ask Him how He feels about the animals there and what He loves about each of them. Lastly, share with Him what you love about the animals. I believe Jesus intends to reveal another part of His heart to you today—through sharing His thoughts about these animals that He loves.

— Ask Him —

- How do you feel about the animals here?
- What do you love about each animal?

Date 71

Will You Run with Me?

Blessed is the one who perseveres under trial because, having stood the test, that person will receive the crown of life that the Lord has promised to those who love him.
—James 1:12

Don't let the title of today's date stop you from participating. Feel free to replace the word "run" with "walk."

Today you and Jesus are going for a short, one-mile run or walk. The point of today's date is to get in the habit of inviting Jesus to be a part of everything you do, no matter if it's big or small. And it also doesn't hurt to set aside a little time to care for the temple (your body) He's given you.

— Ask Him —

- When did you exercise when you were here?

Date 72

Poets, Poems, and Promises

Teach these new disciples to obey all the commands I have given you. And be sure of this: I am with you always, even to the end of the age.
—Matthew 28:20 NLT

Roses are red, violets are blue, my life would completely suck without you! Today, you're going to sit down and write a poem to Jesus. It can be as deep or as light and fun as you'd like. Try to incorporate things that are unique to your relationship with Him, such as things you've experienced while on your dates together. Once you complete the poem, I want you to recite it to Him.

— Ask Him —

- Why was poetry so meaningful to King David?

Date 73

I Spy

The LORD is my shepherd, I lack nothing.
—Psalm 23:1

As a child, did you ever play *I spy* on long car rides with your family? I did, and I remember always trying to "spy with my little eye" something no one else could see. Today, you and Jesus are going to play *I spy* together, but it won't be exactly like the game you played as a child.

I want you to find a quiet, peaceful place to "be" with Jesus, and I want you to ask Him what He spies when He looks at you. When I did this date with Jesus, I was completely wrecked. When I asked Him what He saw when He looked at me, He said, "I spy with my eye resilience, integrity, joy, perseverance, and humility." Knowing what Jesus saw when He looked at me changed what I saw when I looked at myself, and I believe it will do the same thing for you.

— Ask Him —

- What do you spy when you see me?

Date 74

Happy Hour!

A cheerful heart is good medicine, but a
crushed spirit dries up the bones.
—Proverbs 17:22

Have you ever met a person who didn't love happy hour? Yeah, neither have I. Today you and Jesus are going to find a place in your area that has a happy hour and hang out over tasty bites and beverages. Feel free to bring your Bible (no shame if it's on your phone 😊), a journal, and/or your laptop or tablet.

As you sit down and enjoy a bite together, ask Jesus who He wants to make happy during this hour. Maybe He wants you to give a bigger tip to your waitress or waiter, pray for the busboy, or give the manager a word of encouragement. This date is less about small bites and more about pouring Jesus's love into someone to make their hour happy!

— Ask Him —

- Show me Bible verses about happiness.

Date 75

Hey, Future Me, Part 2

The Lord is my best friend and my shepherd. I always have more than enough.
—Psalms 23:1 TPT

Do you remember the letter you wrote to yourself with Jesus on date 24 of this book? Well, today you're going to go find it and reread it. I want you to take a moment and remember how your relationship with Jesus was back then, and how it's evolved since you began going on these dates with Him. Take a moment to speak to the version of yourself that wrote the letter, and celebrate the version of yourself who's reading it today.

— Ask Him —

- Where have you noticed growth in my life?

Weekend

Date 76

Exploring the City

You are the light of the world—like a city on a
hilltop that cannot be hidden.
—Matthew 5:14 NLT

Today you and Jesus are going on an invigorating adventure around the city. You might choose to explore parts of the city you live in that you've never seen, or you can head to a city nearby to explore. Allow yourself to embrace and truly experience the spontaneity of Jesus. If he prompts you to stop somewhere, do it. If He says not to enter a certain city, listen. The purpose of today's date is to experience the beauty of discovering the world with Jesus. There are so many hidden gems He wants to show you!

— Ask Him —

- Which part of the city should I start with?

Weekend

Date 77

Camping or Glamping?

*In his hand are the depths of the earth, and the
mountain peaks belong to him. The sea is his,
for he made it, and his hands formed the dry
land.*
—Psalm 95:4–5

Today you and Jesus are going camping (or glamping, if you're anything like me). It really doesn't matter how you camp; whether in a tent, RV, vacation rental, or cabin, this will be a great opportunity to get away from technology, relieve some stress, and relax in nature. I encourage you to bring friends and family along for this adventure.

Sometimes we hear Him best when we remove ourselves from the hustle and bustle of our everyday lives and sit in the splendor of nature. See some camping activities on the next page.

Ask Him:

- What season of life am I in?
- How should I be praying?

CAMPING ACTIVITIES

- Make s'mores
- Roast hotdogs
- Fish
- Canoe or kayak
- Tubing
- Hike
- Play cornhole
- Birdwatch
- Nature gather (pine cones, rocks, flowers, etc.)
- Have a camping scavenger hunt
- Swing in a hammock
- Listen to nature
- Take a nap
- Stargaze
- Read a book
- Shoot off fireworks
- Sing campfire songs
- Dance around the fire

Date 78

Pinterest Pass or Pinterest Fail?

You know that when your faith is tested, your endurance has a chance to grow.
—James 1:3 NLT

Pinterest is an inspiration-sparking, image-based social media network that is great for finding ideas for recipes, home and style ideas, and craft projects. Today you and Jesus are going to recreate a Pinterest idea or task you've been dying to attempt.

Have fun with this date. Give yourself room for grace as you and Jesus make an attempt at something new. Whether you pass or fail isn't as important as having fun!

— Ask Him —

- What would you love to see me try to make?

Date 79

Creating Music and Memories

The Lord is my strength and my shield; in him
my heart trusts, and I am helped; my heart
exults, and with my song I give thanks to him.
—Psalm 28:7 ESV

Today you and Jesus are going to create a worship song together. Before you tell me all of the reasons why this isn't in your lane, ministry, or realm of expertise. I want to tell you that Jesus isn't looking for or requiring perfection from you. He just wants you to trust Him enough to say yes and step out on the water. So pull out the Notes section on your phone, or grab a pad and paper, and start writing! There is a song inside of you that the earth longs to hear, and I'm sure it will be a #1 hit in heaven.

— Ask Him —

- Give me the words to say what I love most about you.

Date 80

Bonding over Bonfires

*John answered them all, 'I baptize you with
water. But one who is more powerful than I
will come, the straps of whose sandals I am not
worthy to untie. He will baptize you with the
Holy Spirit and fire.'*
—Luke 3:16 NLT

Tonight you and Jesus are going to bond over a bonfire.
You can create a bonfire in your backyard or go to a place
in your area that has outdoor firepits. Before you go, I
want you to reread two of your favorite Bible stories from
the New Testament about Jesus. When you start your
bonfire tonight, I want you to share with Him what set
your heart on fire from those stories.

— Ask Him —

- Which Bible story should I reflect on this week?

Date 81

Playing at the Park

As the Father has loved me, so have I loved you.
Abide in my love.
—John 15:9 ESV

Today you and Jesus are going on a date to the park! Allow your inner child to shine through on this date. Jump on the swings, head down the slide, or attempt to conquer the monkey bars. The purpose of today's date is to remind you that your childlike nature is acceptable, admired, and loved deeply by Jesus.

— Ask Him —

- What did I love doing as a child that I stopped doing, and how can I get that childlikeness back?

Date 82

Party Hardy!

There is a time for everything, and a season for every activity under the heavens: ... a time to weep and a time to laugh, a time to mourn and a time to dance.
—Ecclesiastes 3:1, 4

If you struggle to celebrate yourself, today's date might be a little uncomfortable for you. Today you are going to sit down with Jesus and ask Him what accomplishments, big or small, you've failed to celebrate; and then you're going to celebrate them. Maybe He wants you to celebrate increased patience as a mom, the fifty-cent raise you received at your job, or the fact that you've been consistent with working out and eating better.

Once you know what you're celebrating, it's time to throw yourself a party. Grab a few balloons, write yourself a card, grab a cupcake, invite a few friends over, and get the party started.

Prayer

Jesus, thank you for reminding me of my accomplishments and teaching me how to celebrate myself in every season. I ask that you would continue to prompt me when it's time to throw myself a mini party and celebrate the things you're doing in my life. Amen.

— Ask Him —

- What should I celebrate most about your design of me?

Weekend

Date 83

Yard Sale Vibes

I have told you these things so that you will be filled with my joy. Yes, your joy will overflow!
—John 15:11

We all have a few things in our home that we can get rid of. It might be those shoes from 2007 that collect dust in your closet, or that blender you never use. Regardless, there are a few items you can sell and make a little extra cash from.

Today you and Jesus are going to go through your house and create a pile of all the things you can get rid of. Once you have it all together, go ahead and create an online yard sale or set one up in your front yard. After you're all done selling your items, ask Jesus the questions below:

— Ask Him —

- What do you want to give me in return for everything I gave?
- What should we do with the money we raised?

Weekend

Date 84

Beautiful Boat Rides

A voice came from heaven: "You are my Son,
whom I love; with you I am well pleased."
—Mark 1:11 NIV

There is something so peaceful about being out on the
water with Jesus, watching the sun glare off the sparkling
blue water, the birds hovering above you, and the cool
breeze on your skin. Today you and Jesus are going for a
boat ride together. Whether you end up in a small canoe
on the lake or gliding down the river on the ferry, I want
you to be as present during today's date as you possibly
can. Try to limit your phone time, and allow your spirit,
body, and soul to be aware of His presence. I believe His
still, small voice wants to speak directly to your heart today.

— Ask Him —

- What would you like to say to my heart?

Date 85

Endless Adventures

*Call to me and I will answer you and tell you
great and unsearchable things you do not
know.*
—Jeremiah 33:3

A life lived with Jesus is a life of endless adventures! Today you and Jesus are going to sit down and plan a trip together. Maybe it's the mission trip you've been wanting to go on for years, that fun trip to Disney World, or the trip to Paris you dreamed of as a young child. You are not planning a pretend trip. You are planning a *real* trip that you and Jesus are actually going to go on in the near future. Ask Him about dates. Look up hotels and flight information, and decide who else is coming along, if anyone. Don't forget to mark your calendar and update your passport!

— Ask Him —

- When are we going?
- How will we pay for this trip?
- Who is coming with us?
- Should we fly or drive?
- What hotel will we stay at?

Date 86

5k Race

Let us run with endurance the race that is set
before us.
—Hebrews 12:1 NASB

You and Jesus are going to train for a 5k race that will be happening in your city. 5k races are perfect for beginners and often support philanthropic causes. On average, four to eight weeks of training are required to help you prepare for the race. You can find upcoming races by visiting your city's local event website.

The goal of this date is to do something physically and emotionally challenging that will demand you tap into another version of yourself. Preparing for this date will require discipline and consistency. Don't doubt how wildly capable you are; you can do this. With every stride, Jesus will be running with you and cheering you on to the finish line.

— Ask Him —

- How was Mary feeling as she ran to tell the others your tomb was empty?

Date 87

Reflection Detection

The Scripture was fulfilled that says, 'Abraham believed God, and it was counted to him as righteousness'—and he was called a friend of God.
—James 2:23 ESV

Today's date is going to be fun, informative, and inspiring. Without any reservations, I want you to ask Jesus which Bible character you remind Him of. Then go read their story, and when you are done, ask Jesus the question below!

— Ask Him —

- Why do I remind you of this person?

Date 88

Word Search Wonders!

*You are a chosen people, a royal priesthood, a
holy nation, God's special possession, that you
may declare the praises of him who called you
out of darkness into his wonderful light.*
—1 Peter 2:9 NLT

Today you're going to complete the word search below.
It's composed of twenty words Jesus uses to describe
you. As you find each word hidden in the sea of letters,

— Ask Him —

- Why is each word significant?

Dates with Jesus!

C	L	O	Y	A	L	W	O	R	T	H	Y	N	P
O	O	R	U	C	H	O	S	E	N	I	R	N	O
M	R	E	E	O	A	L	Y	R	E	I	V	A	D
P	I	W	L	S	U	O	U	A	L	H	I	D	I
A	G	E	I	B	I	O	S	U	D	O	C	V	L
S	H	E	W	T	A	L	F	O	T	N	T	E	I
S	T	O	D	E	T	I	I	R	E	E	O	N	G
I	E	U	A	E	T	Y	L	E	E	S	R	T	E
O	O	R	O	U	M	I	N	E	N	T	I	U	N
N	U	W	A	N	T	E	D	L	R	T	O	R	T
A	S	E	C	S	U	O	E	G	A	R	U	O	C
T	B	D	R	U	E	E	N	D	O	B	S	U	E
E	R	B	E	L	O	V	E	D	E	I	Y	S	N
A	A	B	S	E	L	O	V	E	R	R	O	H	T

COURAGEOUS
CHOSEN
BELOVED
LOVER
RESILIENT
REDEEMED
WANTED
WORTHY
RIGHTEOUS
COMPASSIONATE
ADVENTUROUS
DILIGENT
LOYAL
WITTY
BEAUTIFUL
HONEST
VICTORIOUS
RELIABLE

Date 89

Mindful Breathing

You bless the godly, O LORD; you surround
them with your shield of love. —Psalms 5:12
NLT

Today you're going to engage in an exercise called mindful breathing. The idea behind mindful breathing is to get you to anchor yourself in the present moment by focusing your attention on your breathing—it's natural rhythm and flow—and the calmness you feel with each inhale and exhale. This exercise will be a great tool to utilize on the days you're feeling stressed or carried away by negative thoughts and emotions.

During this date, as you ground yourself, allow your spirit to become aware of God's shield of love that surrounds you.

Exercise: Stand, sit, or lie down comfortably, and inhale for 3 to 6 seconds through your nose and exhale for 3 to 6 seconds out through your mouth. Do this for 30 seconds to 15 minutes!

— Ask Him —

- Why is anchoring myself in the present moment so important?

Weekend

Date 90

Catch a Play

Devote yourselves to prayer, being watchful
and thankful.
—Colossians 4:2 NLT

Today you and Jesus are going to catch a play in your area. Search your local listings for all upcoming plays. Whether it's a high school play, college play, or local church play, allow yourself to catch whatever revelation Jesus is throwing your way.

The point of this date is to continue learning how to abide in Him. This means refusing to experience any part of your day, week, month, or year without Him.

— Ask Him —

- I'm looking back at the last event I was part of. Will you show me where you were and what you were doing?

Weekend

Date 91

Team Work Makes the Dream Work

The body is not made up of one part but of many.
—1 Corinthians 12:14

Have you ever heard that team work makes the dream work? Well, it's true. Jesus created us with the idea of community in mind. We were never meant to walk through life alone.

Today's date will challenge your competitive side and also your ability to move in sync with the body. You and Jesus are going to create or join a social sports team and play a game. Whether it's the softball team at your church, a basketball game at your local gym, or competitive tic-tac-toe on the sidewalk, create a good team and give the game your best effort.

— Ask Him —

- What are you teaching me through this activity?

Date 92

Bold Bucket Lists

The wicked run away when no one is chasing
them, but the godly are as bold as lions.
—Proverbs 28:1 NLT

Have you ever created a bucket list? Simply put, a bucket list is a compiled list of goals, dreams, and aspirations that you would like to accomplish during your lifetime. Examples of bucket list goals can be skydiving, visiting the Great Wall of China, retiring early, or attending the Olympics.

Your list should be specific to the things you hope to accomplish before you depart this side of heaven. Take a second and ask yourself what sets your soul on fire. Be sure to create your list with Jesus! There might be things He wants you to do that you've never thought of.

— Ask Him —

- What should I include on my bucket list?

Date 93

Here Comes the Bride

*Let us be glad and rejoice, and let us give honor
to him. For the time has come for the wedding
feast of the Lamb, and his bride has prepared
herself.*
—Revelation 19:7 NLT

Ques music Here comes the bride, here comes the
bride.... Today you and Jesus are going to share your
wedding vows with each other. To date you've gone on
ninety-two fun, spontaneous dates with Him, and I think
it's time to take your relationship to the next level.

In the Bible, we're considered the beautiful, spotless
bride of Christ. And I don't know about you, but I've
never been to a wedding where the bride and groom
didn't share their vows. Take a few minutes, hours, or
days to write your vows to Jesus. Allow yourself to recall
all of the wonderful experiences you've shared. Then
read your vows to Him, and allow Him to read His vows
to you. I recommend grabbing your journal and jotting
down His vows so you can always go back and reread
them.

Tell Him

- I do.

Date 94

WILD CARD DATE!

So we have come to know and to believe the
love that God has for us. God is love, and
whoever abides in love abides in God, and God
abides in him.
—1 John 4:16 ESV

A wild card date means that you and Jesus get to choose together what you do today! You can walk your dog, write your grocery list, go shopping, or grab dinner. You have two requirements: 1) Make it fun, 2) Make it memorable!

— Ask Him —

- What did you enjoy most about our spontaneous wild card date?

Date 95

Soaking Session

Here's what I've learned through it all: Leave
all your cares and anxieties at the feet of the
Lord, and measureless grace will strengthen
you.
—Psalm 55:22 TPT

Today you're going to enjoy a time of soaking in the presence of Jesus. When you spend time immersed in the presence of Jesus, your life completely changes. Soaking is a time to receive from Jesus, rest in His love, and be renewed by His peace.

Below you will find a few simple tips to help you make the most of your date with Him.

— Ask Him —

- What did I receive from you during our soaking session?

SOAKING

• Get quiet and comfortable: Soaking is about resting, so try to get as comfortable as you can. Some people soak on the floor with a pillow or on a couch.

• Play some relaxing music: Music really helps your mind to focus. Put on some worship music that is relaxing for you.

• Welcome the Holy Spirit: Simply pray "I welcome you Holy Spirit." He's ready and waiting to give you what you need.

• Get rid of distractions: Put your phone on silent, close your laptop, go to a room where there isn't a pile of laundry to fold.

• Listen to what Jesus has to say: Jesus might speak to you through words, pictures, memories, or Bible verses.

• How long should I soak?: Some experienced soakers suggest that your mind won't fully switch off until you've been resting for fifteen minutes. Let yourself be led by the Holy Spirit. It will take time to build up stamina.

Date 96

The Perfect Playlist

I will sing to the Lord as long as I live; I will
sing praise to my God while I have my being.
—Psalm 104:33 TPT

Today you and Jesus are going to create the ultimate playlist to jam out to when you're cleaning the house, exercising, road-tripping, or worshiping. You might add as many songs and genres to this list as you would like. My only request is that you and Jesus choose every song together. This will be His and your unique, soul-stirring playlist.

I've added a song suggestion list on the next page.

— Ask Him —

- Which worship song inspires my soul to worship most this week, and why?

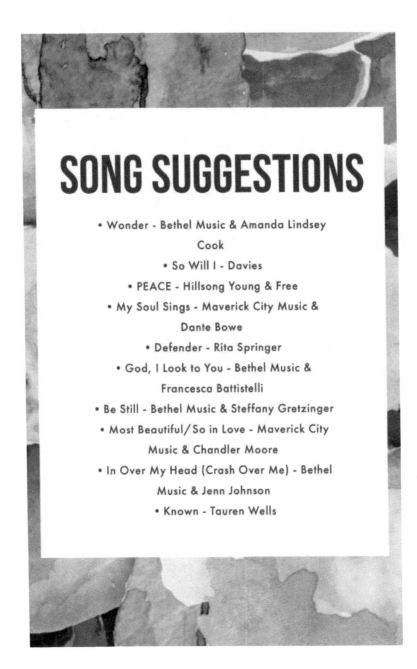

SONG SUGGESTIONS

- Wonder - Bethel Music & Amanda Lindsey Cook
- So Will I - Davies
- PEACE - Hillsong Young & Free
- My Soul Sings - Maverick City Music & Dante Bowe
- Defender - Rita Springer
- God, I Look to You - Bethel Music & Francesca Battistelli
- Be Still - Bethel Music & Steffany Gretzinger
- Most Beautiful/So in Love - Maverick City Music & Chandler Moore
- In Over My Head (Crash Over Me) - Bethel Music & Jenn Johnson
- Known - Tauren Wells

Weekend

Date 97

Botanical Garden Bliss

*As the soil makes the sprout come up and a
garden causes seeds to grow, so the Sovereign
LORD will make righteousness and praise
spring up before all nations.*
—*Isaiah 61:11*

Today, you and Jesus are headed to a botanical garden. This is a garden dedicated to the collection, cultivation, preservation, and display of a wide range of plants labeled by their botanical names. Botanical gardens are typically quiet and very peaceful. Walk around and talk to Jesus about every plant you see that catches your attention.

— Ask Him —

- How does the life of a plant reflect my life with you?

Weekend

Date 98

Horseback Riding

*I looked, and behold, a white horse! And its
rider had a bow, and a crown was given to him,
and he came out conquering, and to conquer.*
—Revelation 6:2 ESV

Today you and Jesus are going horseback riding together.
When you ride a horse, you're trusting your safety to a
twelve-hundred-pound animal. At the same time, you're
learning that the horse trusts you enough to let you climb
on his or her back.

Search for a stable near you that offers horseback riding.
Search for a Groupon coupon code if needed. Schedule
your appointment and enjoy a date full of adventure and
excitement.

— Ask Him —

- What do I need to know or experience in order to
  trust you more?

Date 99

To Post or Not to Post, That Is the Question

Encourage each other and build each other up,
just as you are already doing.
—1 Thessalonians 5:11 NLT

Okay, today's date is going to be very different from any of the other dates you've done with Jesus thus far. Today Jesus wants to set you free from fear of man's opinion.

Ask Jesus what testimony He wants you to share on one or all of your social media platforms. Maybe He wants you to share about overcoming an eating disorder, breakthrough in finances, or increased intimacy in your marriage. Whatever it is, ask Him what to say and how to say it, and then create your post and share it with your friends. I believe someone is going to be transformed because of your transparency.

— Ask Him —

- Why is my testimony needed?

Date 100

Hope, Happiness, and Healing

O LORD my God, I cried to You for help, and
You healed me.
—Psalm 30:2 BSB

Everyone's journey to healing is different, but one thing we all have in common is that Jesus never leaves us alone in our sorrow. He continually chooses to go on the journey with us. Whether the ailment is physical, mental, spiritual, or emotional, Jesus wants to bring deep healing to you. Life is a battle of learning to unlearn and growing to ungrow. Grab your journal, sit down with Jesus, and ask Him the questions below.

— Ask Him —

- What do you want to heal in me?
- How would you like to heal it?

Answers

1. Bethlehem
2. 27
3. 6
4. Adam
5. Eve
6. 40
7. A rainbow
8. 12
9. A coat of many colors
10. Put him in a basket in the river
11. A burning bush
12. 10
13. By the Red Sea
14. Mt. Sinai
15. Saul
16. The lion's den
17. Mary
18. John the Baptist
19. Carpenter
20. Sea of Galilee
21. Nazareth
22. 12
23. John 11:35, Jesus wept
24. Because His friend Lazarus died
25. Five loaves of bread and two fish

26. Wash their feet

27. Jar of expensive perfume

28. Judas Iscariot

29. Peter

30. Love God with all your heart, mind, soul, and strength

About the Author

Stephanie Burrel is the founder of Beloved Be Free, a nonprofit dedicated to empowering young women in their identity. She is a passionate writer, graduate student, singer, and dog mom who loves to see people live a life lavished in freedom and love.

Stephanie received her BA in communication from Southern New Hampshire University in 2018 and is currently obtaining her MA in clinical mental health counseling from Liberty University.

Stephanie believes that the greatest thing we can do in life is to know God and make Him known. Through her own life experiences, she's found that true wholeness starts with healing. Stephanie is on a mission to see every person she encounters live the life they were truly created for.

Stephanie currently resides in Houston, Texas, where the heat is unbearable and the food options are endless.

CONTACT

Instagram: @officialstephaniealexis

Facebook: Stephanie Alexis Burrel

Email: stephaniealexisauthor@gmail.com

Website: www.Stephaniealexis.net

Can You Help?

Reviews are everything to an author because they mean a book is given more visibility. If you enjoyed this book, please review it on your favorite book review sites and tell your friends about it. Thank you!

Other Books by Stephanie

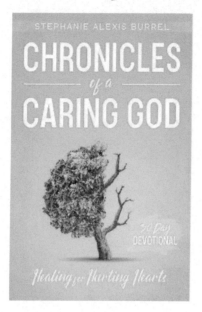

GOD SEES YOU! Know the power, joy, and peace of being heard and seen by God.

In *Chronicles of a Caring God,* readers embark on a personal restorative journey where they encounter Jehovah-Rapha, the God who heals.

The pages of this book express the caring nature of God and His desire to restore every hurting heart. Whether recovering from childhood trauma, divorce, the loss of a child, or life's unmet expectations, this spiritually rejuvenating book creates a safe place for readers to experience deep healing and take back their lives.

Experience new hope, clarity, and freedom today!

Made in the USA
Coppell, TX
05 November 2022

85802831R00075